RIGHTS OF WOMEN

29325

Mandy Wharton

GLOUCESTER PRESS
London : New York : Toronto : Sydney

4 RIGHTS OF WOMEN

INTRODUCTION

There is an old Turkish proverb which says "women are all one nation". It's a point of view held by many feminists today who believe that women all over the world have a great deal in common as friends, wives, mothers, lovers and sisters. Most feminists would argue that women lose out in practically every country just because they are women. They earn less money, have a lower status in society, do more work and often have fewer rights than men.

But what does it mean to talk of the "rights of women"? Most people assume that women have the right to be treated equally in society. But equal to whom? Men are not all treated equally and many women are far more privileged than many men. What does equal treatment imply?

This book will look at the rights that have been fought for by women, and by men for women, and at the way women's role has changed over the years as a result of winning some of these rights. Most of the book will be about women in Western industrial countries, but comparisons and examples from the Third World will be given as much as possible. It is important to remember that women in different societies need different things, and that women within any society do not agree about the rights they have or should have.

Making a judgement about how far women have achieved equality depends largely on your point of view. Have women come a long way or have they got a long way to go? Perhaps after reading this book you will be able to make up your own mind.

"Women comprise over half the world's population, work twice the hours of men, earn one tenth of the income and own one hundredth of the property." In the Third World, the inequality of women stems to a large extent from mass poverty.

6 RIGHTS OF WOMEN

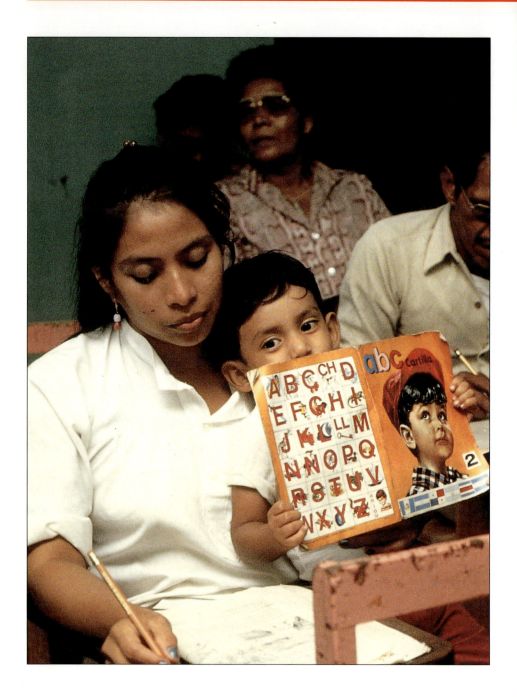

CHAPTER 1

EDUCATION

Two-thirds of the world's illiterates are women, but since the 1960s many self-help groups, literacy schemes and courses have been set up, often by women themselves.

Traditionally, the education of girls and women was about making them into better wives and mothers, and, more recently, about training them for traditional female work. But now education is recognised worldwide as a vital means of gaining access to work and social status, and as ideas about women's equality become more accepted, education in some countries has been concerned with giving girls the same opportunities as boys.

Schooling
During this century girls gradually won the right to receive the same number of years schooling as boys. In the industrialised world they participate in compulsory schooling at the same rate as boys.

> "It was only because we kicked up a fuss in the 3rd year that they let us do things like woodwork and metalwork. Before it was just for the boys."

Since women in the industrialised world have won an equal right to education, their attention has turned to the type of education they get. Some parents and teachers still believe that girls shouldn't do certain subjects, or stay on at school after the compulsory age. For example, it is widely believed that girls are incapable of studying science subjects. In Britain in 1982, boys constituted 73 per cent of national exam entries in physics, 95 per cent in technical drawing and 99 per cent in metalwork. Similarly some people believe boys shouldn't do certain subjects like learning to cook or do needlework.

So are girls and boys different?

Research has shown that boys demand more attention than girls, and that they get more attention from teachers even if they don't demand it. From an early age boys and girls are given different toys to play with, read books where they don't see women working in certain jobs or see men doing housework. The pattern is set very early on. The route through school can be very different for boys and for girls, and this is important for their later life.

Increasingly girls do have the opportunity to choose to follow a science-based education. Yet in Britain in 1982 73 per cent of national exam entries in physics were from boys.

> "We were encouraged to do sciences – the boys treat us equally, they treat us as one of the lads."

Higher education

The proportion of girls who stay on past the minimum leaving age is increasing, but it is still fewer than that of boys.

> "The careers officer sort of had the attitude, jobs for the girls, jobs for the boys. She told some of my mates they were better off being housewives."

The further up the educational ladder you go, the fewer young women you meet. Women were denied entry into university until recently, and even if they could study there, they were not entitled to accept a degree. But since the Second World War, dramatic enrolment increases have occured throughout the world and today women form 40 per cent of university students worldwide.

Harvard opened its doors to women in 1894. Now women are 50 per cent of graduates in the United States' universities. But women students tend to be concentrated in specific subjects such as education.

In the Soviet Union and Eastern Europe, women are 50 per cent of students, in the United States 50 per cent, in Britain 36 per cent, in Japan 33 per cent, in India 25 per cent and in African countries an average of 22 per cent. The type of education girls are receiving is also beginning to change too: there has been an increase in technical school places taken by women and policies to encourage girls into technical and engineering subjects are succeeding in some countries. There has also been a mushrooming of "second chance" courses for older women to upgrade their skills if they missed out on education when they were younger.

> "My parents were really against me going to university, my mother believed it was a total waste of time as I would 'get married and give up work'. But I had other ambitions too, and I won."

The education revolution – right to literacy

In the Third World, female enrolment in primary education is 65 per cent of boys' and in secondary education it is 37 per cent of boys'.

> "Here in rural India girls are removed from school as soon as they can do housework, they never go to secondary school."

Two-thirds of the world's illiterates are women and in 17 countries over 90 per cent of women are illiterate. Women themselves have recognised the importance of education and have set up their own self-help groups, literacy schemes and courses. Women are catching up with men in the literacy stakes and in all other areas of education.

CASE STUDY

Sonia had always done well at school. She worked hard and quietly, never causing any trouble. She went to an ordinary school, she thought it was alright with reasonably friendly teachers.

In the first two years Sonia did especially well at maths and science. In the third year she started going out with a fifth-year boy who was thought to be a rebel, a bit anti-school. Sonia didn't do so well that year, spending more time on her make-up than on her homework! But she had a good time. When it came to the time of choosing examination subjects, Sonia chose to study languages. She had always wanted to be an air-hostess and thought that the languages would come in useful. But she wanted to keep up the science subjects too, but her careers teacher said there was no point. During the next two years Sonia changed quite a lot. She went to Spain one year and decided that being an air hostess was boring. In the fifth year she had to spend some time in hospital with appendicitis. The doctor who treated her was a woman and Sonia had thought her very nice. An idea began in Sonia's mind – perhaps she would like to be a doctor.

When she got back to school, she went to see her careers teacher who said "But you haven't got the sciences. And anyway the competition is tremendous." Sonia talked to a few other people, including her parents, who weren't very encouraging either. When it came to making choices for final school exams, Sonia decided to do the subjects she was best at. She really regretted having given up sciences so she decided to see if she could get into medical school without them. The careers teacher, who was still putting pressure on her, said "I can't see you getting into medical school, and anyway Sonia, I don't think you're the doctor type." Sonia found a medical school where she could do a foundation science course. They accepted her as a student on the basis of the good

CASE STUDY

grades she achieved in her exams. Sonia found medical school to be very hard work. After a few months her parents accepted her decision and began to support her and even feel proud of their daughter.

Eventually Sonia qualified and found a job in a hospital. She also got married although she was worried about how to fit in this demanding job with its long hours with having children. She realised that she had achieved a lot given the hostile forces against her, and knew she would be able to face up to future challenges to herself as a doctor. Everyone was proud of her, and her school asked her back to give a talk.

14 RIGHTS OF WOMEN

CHAPTER 2

WORK

> The jobs women do tend to mirror their domestic responsibilities or rely on nimble fingers. This work is boring, repetitive and badly paid. In many work places there are no men with whom to demand equal pay.

Today, millions of women are in paid employment outside the home – in fact, it has been estimated that one third of all households in the world are solely dependent on a woman's income. Women's wages are increasingly necessary for family survival and most women who work outside the home do so for the same reason as men – because they have to. But women also want to work for personal and social reasons. Having a paid job gives a sense of worth and self-confidence, providing social contact and stimulation as well as a measure of economic independence.

> "What will I be doing in ten years time? Well, I suppose I might be married with kids, but I'll still be working. I want to be a nurse, and I'm not going to give that up – it's what I've always wanted to do."

In the world as a whole, women are 35 per cent of the total workforce. In the industrialised countries this proportion is around 40 per cent and 32 per cent in the Third World. However, much of this work is done on a part-time basis, and in the Third World a lot of work which would be classified as agricultural elsewhere is seen as unpaid domestic labour.

Patterns of women's employment

Men and women tend to be concentrated in very different kinds of work. In every country and every region of the world there are jobs that are specifically defined as women's work. The types of work considered suitable varies over time and between cultures. In Africa women perform 60-80 per cent of the agricultural work and overall women produce at least half the world's output of food. In Ghana women do 88 per cent of the trading, in rural China 90 per cent of cotton and silk-weaving is done by women.

> "I went for a job as a paper sorter. The man interviewing me refused to employ me. They said the job was more suited to a woman because it was boring, repetitive work which a woman wouldn't mind doing."

In the industrialised countries women are found in a much narrower range of occupations than men. Mining is considered unsuitable for women in Europe, but in 19th century Britain women worked in the mines in large numbers. They do so today in South Africa and in the United States. During the Second World War, women were

Dr Sally Ride was the United States' first female astronaut. But her achievements were frequently trivialised in the newspapers. One had the headline "What our girls would pack for orbit."

trained as welders and steelworkers in Britain, but had to give the jobs back to the men at the end of the war. They were encouraged to go back to their "natural" work as mothers. Despite laws against sex discrimination, mostly introduced during the United Nations (UN) Decade for Women, few women work as engineers, plumbers, managers or lorry drivers, just as there are very few male secretaries, sewing machinists or domestic cleaners. This is called occupational segregation by sex. In fact the proportion of engineers who are women varies from about 5 per cent in Africa and Western Europe, to about 25 per cent in Eastern Europe.

The jobs women do tend to mirror their domestic responsibilities – servicing, cleaning, caring and catering. These jobs are defined as being of low skill and low status and are characterised by low pay and little security. Two-thirds of European working women have jobs in the service sector.

High flyers?
Some women do make it to the top. They own companies, hold key positions in government or in business. Yet many of these women have experienced male reluctance to accept their full value and capabilities. One woman who wanted to start her own company was refused a loan by a bank that assumed she was an unrealistic risk simply because she was a woman. Ironically the same bank was prepared to offer the loan to her brother despite the fact that he was unemployed and had been declared bankrupt some years previously.

In the United States women entrepreneurs are seeking new legislation which would help them to set up in business and overcome the short-sighted bank attitudes.

> "If you can manage a family budget, you already know something about how to run a business."

Equal pay

If women's work received equal pay and status to men's, there would be less cause for concern. Despite equal pay legislation there is not yet a country in the world where women's average wages are on a par with men's. The United States introduced the first Equal Pay Act in 1963, but the situation there is worse than in many other countries. For example, in manufacturing industries, women earn on average 58 per cent of men's wages

Many prestigious jobs like working in the stock exchange are gradually being opened up to women. Women have been pilots since 1963, firefighters since 1976 and doctors since 1849.

(that is they are paid just over half as much money for the same number of hours). In Japan they get 43 per cent, in Britain 69 per cent, in Australia 76 per cent and in Sweden 90 per cent.

Equal pay laws have had limited effect because they generally only apply to where men and women are doing the same work. But most women work in workplaces where there are no men at all to be compared with. Recently, however, women have been campaigning for "equal pay for work of equal value".

Jobs which are carried out mainly by women are badly paid especially in areas of employment where there are few men. Most shop assistants in big stores are women – and low paid.

"I don't think of myself as a servant or a sex symbol. I think of myself as someone who can save lives, who knows how to open the door of a jumbo jet when it's upside down in the water in pitch blackness."

In the United States, for example, legal secretaries have won the right to be compared to carpenters,

clerical workers to truck drivers. In the European Court in 1988 a 25 year old cook at a British shipyard (Julie Hayward) won equal pay with the men working as fitters, painters and insulation technicians in the shipyard. Men have traditionally argued that women's jobs are paid less because they are less skilled. It seems to be more that women's jobs are undervalued and defined as less skilled simply because they are done by women!

Part-time work

Because of their domestic commitments, married women form the bulk of part-time workers throughout the world. In Britain, for example, 41 per cent of employed women but only 2 per cent of employed men work part-time. This means they lose out on sickness, holiday and pension benefits and employment protection legislation. Their career prospects are also reduced.

> "The part-timers are older married ladies who do the accounts. They sort out their hours to suit school holidays. They don't want responsibility or promotion, they just come in for something to do and for pocket money. So we give them the boring work the full-timers wouldn't do."

Unemployment

Statistics on women's unemployment often underestimate the problem. Research in Europe indicates that only 42 per cent of women who have lost their jobs or who are looking for work ever register as unemployed. This is because women, particularly married women, are not entitled to benefits.

Women's jobs are more vulnerable as they are more likely to be part-time, temporary or casual. The introduction of new technologies into offices and factories has displaced a lot of women workers. But, ironically, in many industries – such as textiles – women are unlikely to be replaced by expensive machines. This is particularly true in the developing world where women workers are seen as docile, industrious and cheap.

> **"Nobody thinks of me as unemployed and when I had a job nobody thought that was important either. I was always John's wife or Susie's mother."**

Housework

In every country of the world there are meals to prepare, clothes and dishes to wash, children to care for and cleaning to be done. In the rural areas of the Third World these tasks are combined with the subsistence agricultural work that every woman does for survival. In the industrialised world insurance companies have calculated the commercial value of a housewife at hundreds of pounds a week.

The number of hours women spend on housework in the industrialised world is calculated at around 50-60 a week, compared to men in the United States who do an average of 1.6 hours a day regardless of whether their partner works. A study of rural villages in five countries of the developing world showed that although men worked between 40 and 75 hours a week, women's workload was always heavier by up to 21 hours per week. In three of the countries the men spent a matter of minutes each day on domestic work. For women in the Third World the workload may be reduced as development continues and poverty is reduced. But attitudes still have to change as they do in the industrialised world if women are to be released, by men, from half the household workload so that they can take full advantage of the educational and work opportunities that are being opened up to them. If men and women do not share the responsibility of housework, the gains some women have made will remain restricted to a privileged few.

One survey of British men found that only 21 per cent had ever washed any clothes and 19 per cent had ever done any ironing.

CHAPTER 3

LOVE, SEX AND MARRIAGE

> The words of a traditional Western marriage ceremony still give women an inferior status but marriage laws are changing to give women equality.

Despite the increasing number of options open to women in the industrialised world, the proportion of women getting married is increasing: in Britain, for example, in 1911 27 per cent of women aged 30-39 were single. That proportion has now dropped to 7 per cent. Women are also getting married younger. Perhaps this increase in the number of marriages is surprising but the fact is most women do get married and most women who get divorced remarry. So why do so many women want to get married? In the Western world marriage still tends to be romanticised – it is often dreamed about as an alternative to a boring job, a solution to life's difficulties and with the hope that the couple will live happily ever after. This naive view can lead to much disillusionment and unhappiness when the reality doesn't quite match the image! But the romantic ideal simply does not explain why most people marry. Love is very important to people, and most want to make a public statement about their love and commitment to each other. We are looking for an alliance with someone who will believe in us, who will be loyal to us and who will help us function in a difficult world. Women feel more secure, more adult and less lonely when married.

Equality and divorce
Women have been demanding, and getting, more equality in marriage for over a hundred years: it was not so long ago that a wife could not sign a hire purchase agreement on "her" washing machine. Until the Second World War, women in Britain in public jobs such as teaching and the civil service

had to give up their jobs on getting married. As women have a more equal role in marriage, these relationships are becoming more rewarding for them. On the other hand, it seems that the more equality women get, the more unstable relationships can become, as traditional expectations are not fulfilled.

Women do not seem to be disllusioned with marriage itself, only with one particular one. Most women marry, and most remarry should there be a divorce.

> "I would have expected that after ten or so years of marriage one wouldn't really have much to talk about any more. But, on the contrary, there's more joy and excitement now than when we first met."

The divorce rate is accelerating in the industrialised Western world and the majority of divorces are initiated by women. Divorce laws vary throughout the world. In many countries it is very easy for either men or women to start divorce proceedings. In others, divorce is illegal, as it is in Ireland. In many Muslim countries, men can divorce women for any unstated reason whilst women have few divorce rights.

Patterns of marriage

In many countries the majority of women are married whilst still in their teens. In the Indian sub-continent and in Africa for example, 58 per cent and 50 per cent of all women are married before their 20th birthday. The official minimum legal age of marriage for girls varies from 12 in some Latin American countries to 22 in China, the only country in the world where it is higher for women than for men. In most Western countries the minimum age is 18.

In many Eastern cultures a young couple's marriage is arranged by the parents. This couple are marrying within the Hindu faith and live in Rajasthan in India.

A free choice

In the Western world, women can choose their husbands, although this choice is limited by social and economic factors. This is a huge change that has taken place in the 20th century, and of great benefit to women. In many countries and cultures, marriages are arranged by the parents. But a girl can usually refuse if she does not like the choice. However, arranged marriages can often be more successful than marriages of free choice .

> "I don't know why people fuss about arranged marriages. My parents didn't know each other before getting married. I know lots of people that get into a mess with their marriages despite choosing their own partners."

In the Western world, some women choose to live with their partners without feeling they have to have their love endorsed by a marriage ceremony. However, even in countries such as Sweden most people who live together do eventually marry. Some women choose to live alone or with other women and sometimes these relationships include sexual love. Attitudes to homosexual and lesbian love vary across time and cultures. In our society in the industrialised world it is still frowned upon though not illegal.

Contraception

Many of the changes in the patterns of women's lives including marriage come as a result of the fact that today women can control their fertility. Previously a woman bore children almost continuously until she was 40-50 years old, and then died, on average, when she was 55. Access to contraception varies enormously worldwide but it is estimated that 54 million women use the Pill. There are obvious problems with some contraceptives but the dangers of most of them are far less than the dangers of abortion or continuous pregnancy. Partly as a result of being free from the worries of an unwanted pregnancy many girls feel pressured into having sex before they want to, and this pressure has been increasing over the last 20 years with the "free-love" era of the 1960s combined with the advent of the Pill. We should not underestimate the huge liberation that contraception has been for women who can enjoy sex without fear of pregnancy. But on the other hand it makes it more difficult to say "no".

Abortion

The availability of abortion also varies worldwide, due to religious, cultural, political and economic factors. The breakdown of the extended family, hostile attitudes to single mothers and the increasing numbers of women who do paid work outside the home have also affected attitudes to abortion. In many countries, the horror, pain and risk involved in trying to deal with an unwanted pregnancy illegally are over. In some countries of Africa, in Iran and in Ireland abortion is illegal. In the Soviet Union it has been estimated that abortions exceed live births by 2 or 3 times.

The abortion argument is very complicated and difficult to resolve. There are those that argue that a woman always has the right to end an unwanted

In many countries the moral issues around abortion are not even considered. In others the question causes strong reactions of all kinds and the law on abortion is frequently challenged. Each attempt to change the law provokes demonstrations and counter-demonstrations.

LOVE, SEX AND MARRIAGE

pregnancy. For others, abortion goes against their whole moral or religious beliefs. Until contraception is available to every woman, abortion, legal or not, is inevitable.

> "'So you want an abortion?' He was sympathetic but matter-of-fact. To my surprise, I shook my head. It was an instant gut reaction which went against the grain of every political and moral belief I had ever held. But from that moment on I was determined that no-one should take my baby."

Being attractive and the beauty industry
Although women do now have the means to control their fertility and have the opportunities to enter education and work, there are many subtle pressures which prevent a lot of women from taking up a more independent lifestyle. Women fear that if they do not appear sexy and feminine, they will not be loved and that a man's needs should come before their own. This message is emphasised by the advertising industry. Women spend $60 million a year on cosmetics. In the United States in 1984, 95,000 breast enlargement operations were performed, the most popular type of cosmetic surgery. A woman's physical appearance is how she is judged and what she is noted for, in a way inconceivable for men. Under this type of pressure, women are seen by men as "sex objects" rather than real people with real feelings.
As society continues to represent women as sex objects, it overemphasises the importance of sex without love.

LOVE, SEX AND MARRIAGE

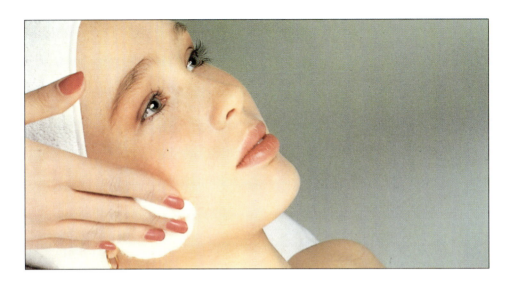

"... with her fringe swept away, she looked sophisticated and sexy. Her coral pink wrapover dress looked comfortable and was as smooth as her interviewing technique."

Women pay fortunes to be beautiful and to fit society's standards. But beauty treatment can be risky: many of us risk cancer to get a tan, whilst others destroy their skins to be paler.

Sex for sale

If women are portrayed as sexual objects, they lose their identity as women and even as people to be respected. Sex becomes easily separated from love. "Playboy" has an annual circulation of over four million copies, but it is soft stuff when compared to some pornography.

Another branch of the sex industry is prostitution, which is illegal in many countries but flourishing worldwide. Sexual violence against women appears to be increasing. One reason for this could be that it is a backlash against the increasing power of women. Another is that women are more prepared to report violence

against them. Violence towards women has always existed, and it is only in the last ten years or so that it is being treated seriously by the law and people in general. Rape is one such crime. The proportion of rapes being reported is increasing, although still estimated at only 10 per cent of those that actually occur. In many states of the United States and in the Soviet Union and in a few other countries, wife rape is also considered a crime. Violence against wives is no longer seen as a private matter. The police are more willing to intervene in situations of domestic violence.

Women fight back

There is no doubt that in practically every country in the world, violence against women, in the form of prostitution, pornography, rape or battering, is a real barrier to women's full and equal rights. The change is coming in the way women are fighting back. In India, Hindu widows no longer have to burn themselves on their husband's funeral pyre. In China girls no longer have to bind their feet to stop them growing, a brutal and painful practice that had kept married women practically immobile. There are still examples of injustices to married women; a campaign is still going on in India to end the dowry system, as husbands are still going unpunished for killing their wives who bring an insufficient dowry and in some Muslim countries women have few rights in marriage. But things are changing and improving.

Hopefully, as women have more choice in when, how and to whom they marry or live with, these relationships will be more equal and loving.

Girls and women involved in prostitution are usually poor, often single parents and sometimes immigrants. Third World women are sometimes lured to the West with a promise of a job and then forced to work as prostitutes.

36 RIGHTS OF WOMEN

CHAPTER 4

CHOOSING TO BE A PARENT

Being a mother and worker go hand in hand in many countries. Women in the Third World are back at work in the fields or fishing a few days after giving birth, their babies on their backs.

A woman's experience of motherhood depends today on how poor she is, where she lives, and her social circumstances. Womens' roles and rights as mothers are changing, as too is the role of men as fathers.

Childbirth

Women's experience of childbirth has changed dramatically with the advent of modern pain-relieving drugs and with improved medical knowledge. As women's status in society has improved, so women have been able to state how they wish to give birth.

> "I wanted to give birth as naturally as possible, with no drugs. They all agreed with this in the hospital. When it came to it, I had to have an emergency caesarian. Thank goodness for modern medicine!"

Many women used to die in childbirth, and in some countries the rate is still high. Less than one half of the world's women give birth with qualified medical assistance at hand. On the other hand, women in industrialised countries have been demanding a move to more "natural" childbirth as it has become increasingly medicalised. The main achievement is that childbirth is increasingly being seen as something women have a right to control.

Motherhood or career?

In many industrial countries, women no longer have to give up their paid work to have children. It would seem that they can have the best of both worlds, the rewards of caring for small children

CHOOSING TO BE A PARENT

and the benefits of working. Certainly, it is in this area that the most radical changes have taken place for women. Maternity laws exist in practically every country in the world, although they differ immensely. Scandinavia and the European socialist countries have the best maternity laws, and women can have paid leave and their jobs are protected. In a few countries, like Sweden for example, the father can take this leave rather than the mother. In practice they don't tend to – a break can damage careers! The United States, on the other hand, is the worst among industrial countries in providing maternity protection – women have to work out their own deals privately with their employer.

In reality, many women do give up their paid

Most women during childbirth have the father of the child or a friend with them. In the industrialised world women are insisting on more control over the birth process.

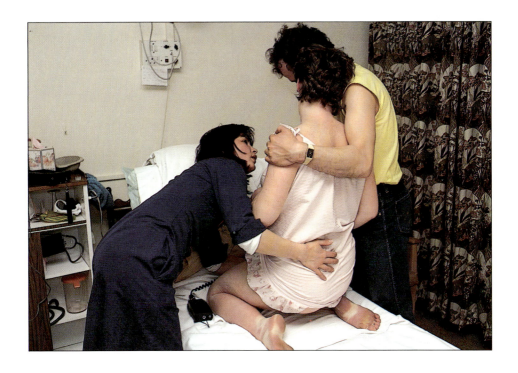

RIGHTS OF WOMEN

work when they have children, partly because of the moral pressure on them to be "good mothers", partly because they find the double load of work and motherhood too much and many women undoubtedly prefer to be at home with their children. Some go back to work when the children go to school, but they are still responsible for the home as well: they have a double load.

Day care allows both parents to carry on working, and is increasingly seen as an important aspect to a child's development too.

"Both my children went to full-time nursery at six months old. It cost practically my whole salary, but it was right for both me and for the children who loved every minute of it."

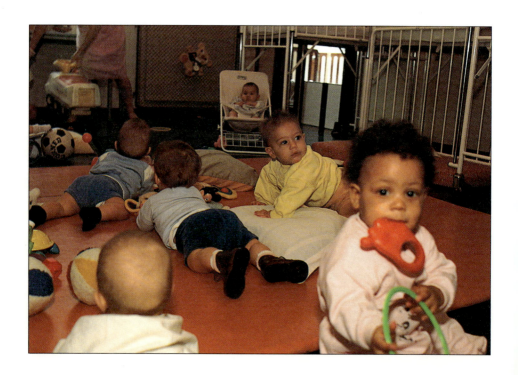

Childcare

Care of one's own children is nowhere officially regarded as "work". In some countries, society has accepted the responsibility of caring for children. For example, in the Soviet Union and Eastern Europe, childcare for pre-school children is provided by the state so that mothers can work outside the home. In the West, Sweden has very good pre-school provision. In the Israeli kibbutzim, children do not live with their parents and are cared for by trained adults. But in most countries mothers, or grandmothers, look after the children before they go to school and there is inadequate provision of nursery and pre-school facilities.

Furthermore women are made to feel guilty at leaving their children with childminders and at nurseries; the children will suffer from "maternal deprivation", they are told. But childcare by individual mothers can be limiting for the child as well as boring and frustrating for the mother.

> "My mum's life is so boring. She cooks the dinner, goes to bed with dad, gets up in the morning and cooks breakfast, cleans the house, and that's all she does all day."

Fathers

Men increasingly have to look after children on their own: with the breakdown of the extended family in the industrial world, widowers and divorced men with custody look after their children. The growth of male unemployment and changing work patterns has meant some role reversal too. Some men voluntarily stay home, but

RIGHTS OF WOMEN

as men usually earn more than women this is not always practical. Men are taking more interest in their children – many men now choose to be present at the births of their children, and many couples share domestic work equally.

The changing role of fathers is slow but very encouraging. Despite the huge advances that have been made in women's role as mothers, motherhood can be a serious brake on the achievement of equality for women. So many advancements depend on women having the time, energy and opportunity of being able to participate equally in all elements of work, political or social life. If men and women took equal responsibility for parenting, then the emotional gains would be great for both, and true equality would be nearer. Children would also benefit from the care of both parents.

Many men are now involved in childcare and discovering that bringing up children is an intense and rich experience. Involvement also means that they discover looking after a child can be frustrating, boring and... exhausting.

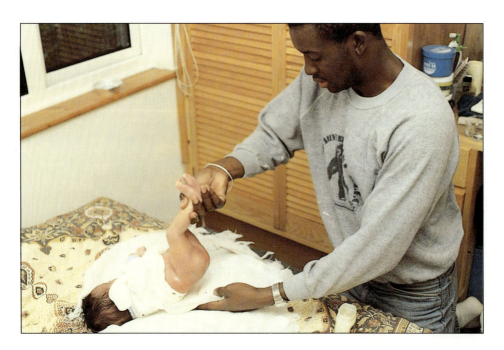

CASE STUDY

Martha, a solicitor, and John, a teacher, both want to have children. Martha is very keen to discuss exactly how they will look after the children – she does not intend to give up her career for a family. All goes according to plan, and a baby girl is born a year later. Martha finds motherhood very rewarding and loves having this chance to be at home. But John finds himself rather distant from baby Ruth. But the summer holidays come and as he spends more time with Ruth he begins to enjoy himself. In September, they both go back to work, Ruth starts with her new childminder but it quickly becomes obvious that she is not happy there. Martha and John discuss all the alternatives open to them. Finally Martha suggests that John could give up his job to look after the baby. John is horrified at the idea at first, but then remembers how much he enjoyed the summer holidays. Eventually, John agrees to stay at home to look after Ruth.

CHAPTER 5

SPORT AND LEISURE

Mount Everest was first climbed by women in 1975. In 1985 a women's team explored this hidden peak in Pakistan. Mountaineering is one sport where men have no advantages over women and most expeditions now include women.

Women have made great headway in breaking into male preserves in the sport and leisure scene -many have not been content to sit on the sidelines. Girls no longer want to experience sports and hobbies secondhand through their boyfriends, like Shelley who spends every Saturday afternoon watching Ian play football, or Jackie who goes down the club every Friday to hear Winston play.

Women in men's sports
There are very few sporting activities that are now barred to women. Girls and women have always gone to football matches, but are not usually thought to have any interest in or knowledge of the game but in fact there are over 235 women's football teams in England alone. In one track club in New York, women have been allowed to compete alongside the men since 1959, and in 1978 Marion Tyger Trimiar was granted a New York state boxing license. These successful entries into men's sporting domains have not been handed over on a plate, they have been fought for. The modern Olympic Games began in 1896, but not until 1926 were women allowed to compete in track events, and then only in five. Women were banned from marathons in the United States until 1972. In 1976 during the all-male Boston Marathon, an official tried to eject Kathy Switzer as she ran, but was thrown to the side-lines by another (male) runner. Women have always had their own sports, which fitted in much more with the traditional view of femininity (except hockey and lacross which are very tough team games). They have never had the same status as men's sports,

although this is changing. In 1970 the Italian Open tennis prize for women was $600 whereas for men it was $7,500, and women have campaigned to make prize money more equal in the face of comments that women are much worse tennis players than men. Billie-Jean King rammed the point home when, after Bobby Riggs proclaimed no woman could beat him, she defeated him in straight sets in 1973.

Sportswomen still have to battle against the sexism which tries to belittle their achievements and define them in a sexual way. But this should not detract from their success as athletes.

> Sports coverage is dominated by male sports but, contrary to appearances, football is one sport where women are beginning to win a place. When will we see a women's football match on the television?

> "Australia's Jan Stevenson was nominated today as the sexiest swinger in golf. Her sinuous body movements remind us of Marilyn Monroe."

Neutral sports

Perhaps the greatest achievements of women have been in the area of individual sports which require different qualities than the traditional team games. Women have made their names in sailing, swimming, skiing, skating, climbing. Mount Everest was first climbed by a woman in 1975 and most expeditions include women. Of course, this tradition dates back to the 19th century when there were several female explorers. In long-distance swimming, women perform equally with, or better than, men. Eight of the ten fastest English channel swims are by women and in 1979 Diana Nyad was in the water 27hours and 38minutes to become the first person to swim from the Bahamas to Florida.

Catching up with the men

The improved opportunities, training, encouragement and incentives over the last 20 years has led to improvements in women's performances. Simple and apparently obvious biological reasons for differential treatment and performances between the sexes are being questioned on the sports field as they are in the workplace.

Time and money – equality?

Most sport covered in the media is men's sport. NBC sports programmes in the United States were

The javelin thrower, Fatima Whitbread, has done a lot for women's sport. But sportswomen with muscles who do not fit the feminine image still have a hard time being accepted as "real women".

monitored for one year. Out of 366 hours of live sport, one hour, the Wimbledon women's final, was of women's sport. In 1980 in major cities in Australia, there were a total of 200 hours of sport in one week, five minutes of which was of women's sport. Obviously there is a long way to go!

Commercial sponsorship goes mainly to male-dominated sports and the earning power of sportsmen is much greater. Budgets for sports are much higher for men. In Eastern Europe where sport is treated equally for men and for women, the results are obvious: in the late 1970s East European women held 75% of top performer places and 86% of world records. As more women become interested in sport and demand more attention, then they are ignored less and less. However, in Third World countries, sport is still very male dominated. In some, religious beliefs would not allow women to display their bodies, in others there simply is not the money to develop sporting facilities.

Other leisure activities – youth clubs
Of course many people have no interest in sport, and pursue other activities in their spare time. Young women tend to meet in each others homes, play records and experiment with make-up. There are often restrictions placed on girls in the evenings by their parents – they don't enjoy the same freedom as their brothers. Youth clubs are one place where young women go, and they are no longer content to sit around while the boys monopolise all the facilities.

> "On Tuesdays when it is mixed, it's chaos. The boys think they own the gym, kicking footballs around all night."

The solution many clubs have found is to have "girls only" nights where girls can gain confidence and form alliances. They feel more able to challenge the boys for space on mixed nights and to then make more equal relationships with them.

Music
Girls are also less content to be passive in the music scene. Many young women now form their own pop groups and there are some mixed bands. It is certainly not an easy scene for girls to break into and many have to work extra hard to be taken seriously for their music.

SPORT AND LEISURE 51

> "When we went on stage for our first gig, the boys started booing and jeering. We hadn't even started playing."

Women have become visible in our culture in a way they rarely were before. Women are being recognised for their talent, not just measured on a scale of how sexy they look. Opportunities for young women to participate in sport and leisure facilities are increasing. Women are challenging their traditional roles. But there is still an enormous amount of sexism around, and older women with families still have their leisure time limited by the disproportionate amount of work that confines them to the home. A heavy workload soon restricts anybody's opportunities.

Bananarama is just one of the many successful women's bands. The number of established women musicians is increasing but many girls still seem to prefer to listen to records or their boyfriends playing.

RIGHTS OF WOMEN

CHAPTER 6

WOMEN AND POLITICS

Women have been allowed to participate in formal politics for 80 years. But few women are in government – as this scene from the United States Senate shows.

It is amazing to remind ourselves that only one hundred years ago women were not considered to be a sufficiently important part of the population to be able to vote. "We the people" excluded 50 per cent of the people. In our history books we learn about democracy in Ancient Greece yet women (and slaves) were not even considered citizens!

Women's political power
New Zealand was the first country to grant all women the right to vote in 1893. Of the industrialised countries, Liechtenstein only gave all women the vote in 1984. In a few countries of the world, such as Bhutan, only men can vote, in a few more, everyone is denied the vote.

Women may be able to vote, but the numbers of women in the national legislatures is very low.

> **"It's a vicious circle. Governments are dominated by men, who do not have women's interests at heart, so nothing changes. Until things change, there will not be more women in government."**

However, the proportion of women is growing. Of course, it doesn't follow that women will automatically fight for women's rights in legislatures. Many women who get to the top see their sex as irrelevant. A female British Labour Party member was asked to stand as leader of the party as no women were standing, and replied "Certainly not! I'm not a woman, I'm a politician."

The Scandinavian countries and Eastern Europe have the best representation of women in their legislatures. The first female politicians were

WOMEN AND POLITICS 55

elected in Finland in 1907, and Finland is top of the league at present with 31 per cent of the parliament being female. Sweden, Denmark and Norway, the Soviet Union and Eastern Europe all have over 20 per cent female representatives in parliament. Britain and the United States have less than 5 per cent. In general, women tend to be much better represented at the local government level and are often to be found in important positions there. Ceylon, (now Sri Lanka) had the first female Prime Minister in 1960, and now there are five female heads of government. The strength of women such as Indira Gandhi, Golda Meir and Margaret Thatcher cannot be denied, whatever we think of their politics. In the case of Indira Ghandhi, she led her country despite the fact that most women in India are denied the right to exercise political power.

Margaret Thatcher, Prime Minister of Britain, is one of the world's leading politicians. However the government she leads is made up almost entirely of men.

> "A woman must do twice as well as a man to be considered half as good. Luckily for us, it's not too hard to be twice as good as a man."

Why still so few women?

The demands made on politicians are enormous, with meetings, all night sittings in parliament, travel and often women's responsibilities towards the family limit their participation in these things. Furthermore women just aren't taken seriously as people with important things to say! But again, things are changing. No one would speak of Mrs Thatcher in a sexual way, she is taken seriously. But somehow she is a token man. It is still difficult for women to be successful and female.

But attitudes to women have changed. In 1937 31 per cent of the American population said they would vote for a suitable woman presidential candidate. In 1976 this had risen to 73 per cent.

Other forms of political power

Political power rests in places other than just parliaments. It rests in big business, in the courts, in the army and in trade unions. Despite the high proportion of women workers in the industrialised world, the proportion of managers who are female is low. In the world as a whole women are only five per cent of trade union officials.

The legal system is also dominated by men, for example women are 3 per cent of judges in Britain, 7 per cent in the United States, 2 per cent in India, but 36 per cent in the Soviet Union.

WOMEN AND POLITICS

> "I'm not very pleased with the union. It's so chauvinistic! I can't even get to union meetings because of the time they hold them, and I pay union dues like the men."

Equal in everything?

Does women's equality mean they should do all the same things as men? If they should, does this include fighting in the army alongside men? In a handful of countries, the latest being the United States, women are allowed into the army in all

If women have equal rights, should they also have equal responsibilities like fighting alongside men in the army?

roles including combat. In civil and revolutionary wars, women are much more likely to be found fighting alongside men, and in some cases these fights are linked with women's role in the society in general. Thus in Vietnam, Zimbabwe, Nicaragua, Angola, to name a few, women have taken an equal part in the armed struggle.

> "If a man is carrying all his equipment and his gun, then the women must do the same. We women were never given anything different from the men."

Political protest

Women have always been involved in protest and in great movements. They have often been ignored by historians. Women's past is currently being rediscovered and history reinterpreted by female, and male, historians. Women are becoming visible again. In the last 20 or so years, women have been very active politically throughout the world, fighting for their rights or against some injustice. Women have helped bring the peace movement more into the public eye.

Women's movements

Women organise themselves in groups ranging from the Housewife Register, World Women's Christian Temperance Union, through to Rape Crisis centres, because they believe that they have special needs as women. The most significant movement has been the women's liberation movement which emerged in the 1960s and which has forced governments to change laws and people to

WOMEN AND POLITICS

change attitudes throughout the world. It has helped many individual women in their difficult lives but there is still a long way to go.

> "I think the role of women has changed a lot since I was born 60 years ago. But when I switch on the television and watch the news, I'm still amazed that nearly every news item is about men. We've got a long way to go."

This conference in Moscow in 1987 is one of the many where women from all over the world meet to plan how to better their rights.

SOURCES OF HELP

If you would like more information about any aspect of women's rights, then write to :
The Equal Opportunities Commission (EOC)
*Overseas House
Quay Street
Manchester M3 3HN
Telephone 061 833 9244*

Information about the position and status of women worldwide is available from:
Change
*29 Great James Street
London WC1N 3ES
Telephone 01 405 3601*

If you think you have suffered from discrimination, or want to check your legal position, then contact:
The Equal Opportunities Commission
(address as above)

National Council for Civil Liberties
(Women's Rights Unit)
*21 Tabard Street
London SE1
Telephone 01 403 3888*

Rights of Women
*52/54 Featherstone Street
London EC1
Telephone 01 251 6577*

For help and information about specific issues, the following addresses may be useful:
National Advisory Centre on Careers for Women (NACCW)
*Drayton House
30 Gordon Street
London WC1H OAX
Telephone 01 380 0117*
NACCW offers consultation and information about careers' education in schools

Women's Health Information Centre and Women's Aid Federation
*52/54 Featherstone Street
London EC1
Telephone 01 251 659810*

British Pregnancy Advisory Service (for all local branches)
*1st Floor
Guildhall Buildings
Navigation Street
Birmingham 2
Telephone 021 643 1461*

WHAT THE WORDS MEAN

adultery when a husband or wife has sex with someone outside the marriage

caesarian abdominal operation to lift out the baby from the womb. Caesar was supposed to have been born this way

chauvinistic a term used to describe men (or women) who treat women as inferior because of their sex

dowry a payment by a woman's family to her husband on marriage

Eastern Europe countries which have a type of socialist system like the one in the Soviet Union. They are East Germany, Poland, Hungary, Albania, Romania, Yugoslavia, Bulgaria and Czechoslovakia

industrialised world countries where industrial labour is the main feature of the economy. Sometimes called the developed world or the advanced world

legislatures the group of people who make the laws of a country, for example, the House of Commons in Britain and the Senate in the United States

socialist a society where there are no large privately owned firms. The state owns everything. Socialist countries believe in the ideal of the equality of all people

subsistence agriculture a term used to describe how a family or group of people grow the food they need to live on

Third World a term used to describe the developing countries, those with an economy based on agriculture

United Nations an organisation of most countries of the world which can discuss problems and disputes between countries. It was set up after the Second World War to try and keep world peace

Index

abortion 30, 32
Africa 11, 17, 18, 28, 30
agricultural work 16-17, 22, 61
army 57-58
arranged marriages 29
Australia 20, 49

battering 35
beauty 32
Britain 8, 9, 11, 17, 20, 21, 26, 46, 54

careers 38-40, 42, 43
childbirth 38, 39
childcare 40, 41, 42
China 17, 28
contraception 29-30, 32

divorce 26-28
domestic work 15, 16, 18, 21, 22-23, 40, 42, 51, 56
dowry 35, 61

equality 5, 8, 25, 42, 57-58

fathers 38, 39, 41-42

higher education 10-11
homosexuality 29

India 11, 28, 35

legislation 18, 19, 20, 21, 25, 26, 27, 30
leisure 50-51
lesbianism 29
literacy 7, 11
love 25, 26, 29, 35

marriage 8, 25-35
maternal deprivation 41
maternity laws 39, 43
media 32, 47, 48
motherhood 8, 37-43
music 50

part-time work 16, 21, 22

rape 35

Scandinavia 20, 29, 39, 41, 54, 55
schools 8-9
sex discrimination laws 18
sexual objects 33-35
Soviet Union 11, 30, 35, 41, 54
sport 45-50
status 5, 8, 18, 21, 25

Third World 5, 11, 16, 22, 37, 49, 61

unemployment 21-22, 41
United States 10, 17, 19, 20, 35, 39, 46, 48, 54

violence 33, 35
voting rights 54

Western Europe 18, 47

Photographic Credits:
Cover and page 55: Frank Spooner; pages 4, 6, 36 and 57: Mike Goldwater/Network; pages 9, 10, 17, 23, 31, 44, 47, 49, 51, 52 and 59: Rex Features; page 13: Franklin/Network; page 14: Laurie Sparham/Network; page 19: Mayer/Network; page 20: Arkell/Network; pages 24 and 27: Zefa; page 28: Robert Harding; pages 34, 39, and 40: Magnum; page 41 and 43: Hutchison Library; page 55.